YBP #3

Setting Good Goals and Making Good Decisions
Through the Eyes in My Heart

YBP

Journey of: _____

(your name)

My Eyes' Journey Youth Battle Plan Series

**Setting Good Goals and Making Good Decisions
Through the Eyes in My Heart**
By
Barbara W. Rogers, Ph.D., Ed.S. and Christian Life Skills, Inc.

Editorial Assistant: Tabetha Mwita

Copyright © 2023 Christian Life Skills, Inc.

Paperback ISBN-13: 978-1-6628-8425-2
eBook ISBN-13: 978-1-6628-8426-9
Printed in the U.S.A.

**"For in Him we live and move and have our being."
Acts 17:28 NKJV**

Xulon Press 555 Winderley Place, Suite 225 Maitland, FL 32751 407.339.4217
www.xulonpress.com

Utilize all the books in the My Eyes' Journey series!

Intro: Seeing God's Good Plans for Me

Book 1: Becoming My Best Self

Book 2: Using My Best Mind

Book 3: Setting Good Goals and Making Good Decisions

Book 4: Knowing God

Book 5: Managing My Sexuality

Book 6: Developing Gifts and Resources

Book 7: Developing Respectful, Responsible Relationships

Book 8: Knowing and Managing My Feelings

Book 9: Managing Communication, Media, and a Healthy Lifestyle

YBP #4

Knowing God

Through the Eyes in My Heart

Barbara W. Rogers, Ph.D., Ed.S.
and
Christian Life Skills, Inc.

YBP #5

Managing My Sexuality

Through the Eyes in My Heart

Barbara W. Rogers, Ph.D., Ed.S.
and
Christian Life Skills, Inc.

YBP #6

Developing Gifts and Resources

Through the Eyes in My Heart

Barbara W. Rogers, Ph.D., Ed.S.
and
Christian Life Skills, Inc.

YBP #7

Developing Respectful, Responsible Relationships

Through the Eyes in My Heart

Barbara W. Rogers, Ph.D., Ed.S.
and
Christian Life Skills, Inc.

YBP #8

Knowing and Managing My Feelings

Through the Eyes in My Heart

Barbara W. Rogers, Ph.D., Ed.S.
and
Christian Life Skills, Inc.

YBP #9

Managing Communication, Media, and a Healthy Lifestyle

Through the Eyes in My Heart

Barbara W. Rogers, Ph.D., Ed.S.
and
Christian Life Skills, Inc.

To Rev. Dr. Ronald E. Peters, thank you for the many doors of opportunity you opened to present Christian Life Skills, Inc. at Pittsburgh Theological Seminary and for your help and support as a CLS Board member.

Acknowledgments

The Christian Life Skills curriculum, with its *My Eyes' Journey Youth Battle Plan* series and *Warriors for Jesus* series and all other resource materials, would not have been possible without the work of numerous persons who have served Christian Life Skills, Inc. in various capacities including: Board of Directors, staff, interns, mentors, tutors, general volunteers, and participants—youth, young adults, adults, and senior citizens. The curriculum was utilized, revised, tested, critiqued, and revised again and again.

Instructions

As a way of being introduced to this book, please follow these instructions:

1. Read the Table of Contents.

2. Read the "Preview" and "Focus" pages.

3. Look through the entire book and the Appendix.

In this way, you will do an assessment of what this book is about. After you complete this introductory process and make an assessment, you can determine your plan of action.

Use the next few pages to begin a process of discussing this book, your plans, and your goals with someone. Choose safe people who care and encourage you to do your best. This will help you succeed.

Table of Contents

A PREVIEW FOR YOU!

Did you know the influences in your life affect your choices?

That's what this book is all about!

Did you know the choices you make now can change everything that happens for the rest of your life?

This book is about planning your goals and making choices that are good for you!

Focus

Good things to remember...

Get Good Information,
Think,
Pray,
Read the Bible,
Then Decide!

Introduction

Throughout your life's journey, God wants to help you see through the eyes in your heart. We call this series of books the "My Eyes' Journey Youth Battle Plan." <u>In the logo for this series, the eyes are enclosed in a heart to remind you that God wants you to see through your spiritual eyes, the eyes in your heart</u>. He wants you to live your life in the best way possible. Life is a journey, and God wants to journey with you!

The My Eyes' Journey Youth Battle Plan series of books will help you see through spiritual eyes, *the eyes in your heart*. The Bible, God's Spirit, God's people, and these books can help you know God's good plans for your life and how He wants you to live.

Your heart, with God's Spirit inside your heart, will guide you. Everyone has trouble and problems in life. When you do have trouble and problems, you can pray and ask for God's help. God's Spirit in your heart,

God's Word, and God's people can help you do what is best, even in a bad situation!

It is often a battle to do what is best and right. We often want to do whatever we feel like doing, but that can lead to more trouble. God wants to be your Best Friend and your Helper all the time! When we struggle to do what we know is best and right, we are in a spiritual battle. This series of books teaches us to have a battle plan to make good choices and live in ways that please God, even when it is difficult.

In each book you will be asked how God has helped you see through the eyes in your heart. You will do activities to help you learn to pray and stay close to God. That will help you with the battles to live your best life close to God by seeing through the eyes in your heart, your spiritual eyes.

Chapter 1
Getting Started

"Trust in the Lord with all your heart,
and lean not on your own understanding;
In all your ways acknowledge Him,
and He shall direct your paths."
Proverbs 3:5&6 NKJV

God Has Good Plans for Me

If I try to see things through the eyes in my heart, God can help me set good goals and make good choices!

My Name: _____

Phone: _____

Email: _____

Below, I checked my goals for living into God's good plans:

__1. Read and discuss this book.

__2. Read a Bible story.

__3. Learn a Bible verse.

__4. List safe people who care and encourage me.

__5. Do activities.

__6. Learn strategies and habits to avoid bad influences.

Signed: _____

Date: _____

Encourager: _____

My Village Action Network Team
(My VT)

I am accountable to these safe people who will help me to know God and be my best self:

1. _____

2. _____

3. _____

Other sources of help and encouragement are...

__ Recreation Center   __ Library

__ After-School Activities __ Hobbies

__ Summer Activities   __ Part-Time Job

__ Health Care Center   __ Church Camp

__ Church Activities   __ Police

Other: _____

Warm-up Activities

During the time you are using this book, you may choose to do some warm-up activities related to the topics. Warm-ups may help you see through the eyes in your heart. Circle the warm-ups you might try, either alone or in a group.

1. Interview two or three people face-to-face or electronically. Ask them which skills and strategies they practice and which danger zones or safety zones are challenges for them.

2. Create a banner, skit, step, song, hand-clap-slide, poem, rap, spoken word, clay model, mime, sculpture, collage, or another project to show what you are learning.

3. Make up a game or puzzle about what you are learning.

4. Prepare questions about topics discussed in this book. Invite a visiting panel to give answers.

5. Watch a movie about your topic.

6. Make a video showing what you are learning.

7. Take a field trip related to what you are learning.

8. Take a walk and try to memorize a Bible verse while walking.

9. Create a series of truthful cartoons on your topic.

10. Make a diary or journal, and write about the battles you win and lose in trying to please God. Brainstorm about ways you could win more battles by staying close to God.

11. Jump rope, dribble a ball, or do sit-ups or jumping jacks while practicing your Bible verse.

12. Prepare and present a two- or three-minute sermon on your topic, applying the Bible to real life now.

13. Create a skit that teaches a vocabulary word.

14. Create a life map, telling about key events. If you go online or go to the library, you can learn about "life maps" and many ways to make your own life map.

Warrior Habits to Practice

The ideas on the next few pages will help you use your best mind so you may have success in life! Read them, and check the ones you understand and the ones you would like to try. As these actions become habits, you will be a strong, skilled warrior with God's blessing in your life.

Reflect – means think for a while.

Use **Initiative** – means take action.

Anticipate – means think ahead.

Be **Accountable** – means that you report to someone the truth about how you are behaving—the good and the bad—in working on a goal, job, or behavior you said you would do.

Influences – the things that affect your thoughts, feelings, and actions. To **guard influences** means to carefully choose people, places, and things that affect your thoughts, feelings, or behavior in positive ways.

Preempt – means you act ahead of time to do things so that there is not a problem or so things work out in a way you control or influence.

Strategies – plans to accomplish a goal. To **develop strategies** means to make good plans so you will reach your goals.

Warriors Get a Grip!*

Worship God at church weekly and in all places
Anticipate and be accountable
Read and live by God's Word as a daily habit
Reflect and pray to live God's way
Initiative – take action to please God in all you do
Open the eyes of your heart
Recognize danger zones; stay safe
See through the eyes of your heart

Get encouragement and help
Educate yourself
Treat your body as God's temple

Accomplish good things for others in safe ways

Guard your heart and mind
Rejoice and worship the Lord by being kind
Influences-choose only good ones
Pray, prepare, and preempt bad influences

*These are spiritual disciplines to practice daily!

Understand the Youth Battle Plan

Check the ideas about the battle plan that you understand and agree with.

___God has good plans for my life.

___Bad influences could keep me away from God's good plans.

___I need to reflect and pray about which influences I allow in my life.

___Good, safe people may help me choose and keep good influences.

___It is a spiritual battle in my mind and heart to say and do the good things that keep me close to God.

___I can preempt bad influences by using my time, my mind, my body, and my spirit in ways that please God.

___I can choose strategies that make me a strong warrior. I will win battles to see through the eyes in my heart and practice thoughts and actions that please God.

___Strategies are good plans that help me reach my goals!

Know the Word!

A Bible verse to learn:

Proverbs 3:5&6 NKJV
"Trust in the Lord with all your heart,
and lean not on your own understanding;
In all your ways acknowledge Him,
and He shall direct your paths."
Proverbs 3:5&6 NKJV

Read this verse 3 times daily. Put a check mark here each time you read it.

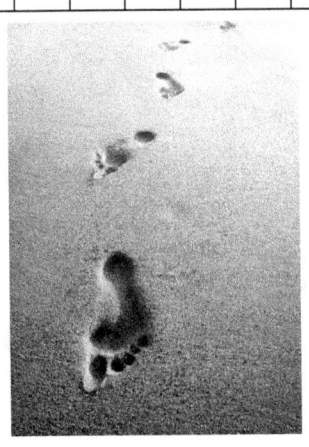

Chapter 2

Strategies for Good Decisions

"Trust in the Lord with all your heart,
and lean not on your own understanding;
In all your ways acknowledge Him,
and He shall direct your paths."
Proverbs 3:5&6 NKJV

Strategic Action Plan I:
Actions for Making Good Choices

Check the ones you plan to do. Once you have accomplished them, write the numbers on the line at the end of this list.

__1.   Memorize Bible verses.

__2.   Read and apply Bible stories.

__3.   Write out and share 4 short-term and 4 long-term goals.

__4.   Tell your team what you do daily to work on your goals.

__5.   List 5 good, safe people who influence your good choices.

__6.   List 5 habits you practice that help with good choices.

__7.   Learn and then name the steps you take to make a good decision.

__8.   Interview and tell stories of 2 real people who made good decisions that were difficult.

continued

___9. List possible consequences of 5 bad decisions and 5 good decisions.

___10. List 5 reasons people get involved with bad choices.

___11. Learn and act out 5 refusal skills.

___12. Learn and act out 5 preemption skills.

___13. Learn and act out 5 problem solving skills.

Which things above did you do?
Write the numbers here:

_____

_____

_____

Strategic Action Plan II:
Focus and Reflect on God's Word

Ask God to open the eyes in your heart so you will understand how He wants you to set goals and make good decisions His way!

Read one or more of the Bible stories listed below. Then create a skit or do another project about one of the stories or part of the story.

The Sons Who Made Choices
Luke 15:11-32

The Boy Who Made Hard Decisions
Genesis 37:2-4, 23-28
Genesis 39:7-10
Genesis 45:3-11, 50:20

Questions to Help You Open and Understand the Eyes in Your Heart

Answer these questions from the Bible stories:

1. What decisions and consequences are in the story?

_____

_____

_____

2. What can you learn from these stories?

_____

_____

_____

3. What changes do you need to make and what habits do you need to practice so that you will behave in the ways these stories teach us?

_____

_____

_____

4. What can you do today to start these changes and habits?

_____

_____

_____

5. Who will you ask to hold you accountable for the changes you need to make and the habits you need to practice?

_____

_____

_____

continued

6. Are you willing to keep praying and asking God to help you obey this part of His Word and all that He shows you? _____

Write your prayer:

_____

_____

_____

_____

_____

_____

_____

_____

_____

_____

_____

Strategic Action Plan III:
Use Discipline, Determination, Discernment, and Resilience

Check the ones you will do.

__1. Make God my Best Friend.

__2. Act out 5 preemption decisions for challenging or tempting situations you may encounter. This will help you to resist pressure and trouble.

__3. Act out and explain ways to manage the battle in my mind and heart when influences could trick me into dangerous, bad decisions instead of good success.

__4. Stay around good, safe people who care about me, respect me, and help me to make choices and reach goals that please God.

__5. Talk with someone about ways to solve difficult problems God's way.

__6. Write out and share the little steps I need to take to accomplish a big goal.

continued

__7. Write and/or talk about how the issues below impact your goals and decisions:

- your interests, abilities
- learning style
- history, culture, family
- temptation
- media and screen time
- stresses and pressure
- strengths and weakness
- likes and dislikes
- gifts and abilities
- all that God has made you to be
- all the blessings God wants to give you.

Chapter 3
You Have Important
Choices to Make!

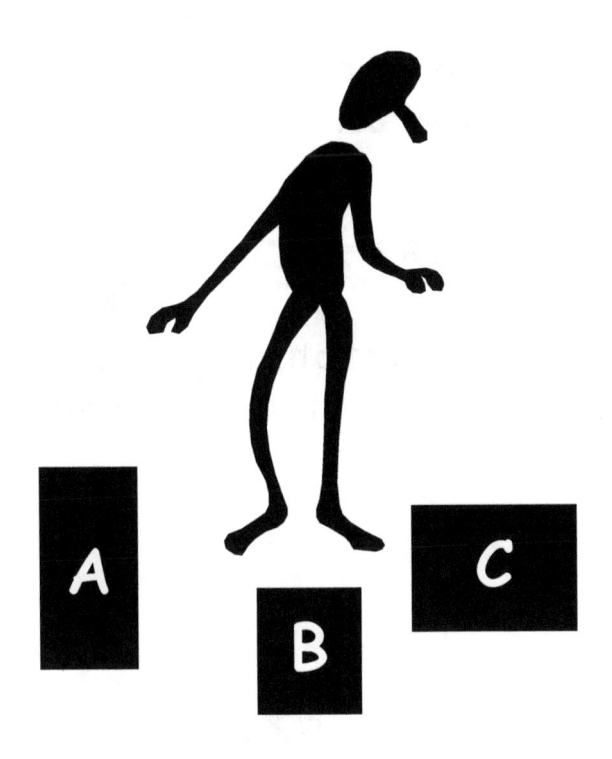

"Trust in the Lord with all your heart,
and lean not on your own understanding.
In all your ways acknowledge Him,
and He shall direct your paths."
Proverbs 3:5&6 NKJV

Strategic Action Plan IV: Be Careful of Risky Business/Danger Zones!

For each issue, check the line to show which you would do.

 **DZ1**

I go along with what other people say and do without thinking about what God wants me to do. ____

Safety Zone **SZ1**

I try to practice habits that help me see through the eyes in my heart and follow God's Word. Before I go with "the crowd," I think ahead about consequences. ____

 **DZ2**

After I do certain things, I wish I had not done them. ___

Safety Zone **SZ2**

I try to think ahead about my choices and not make quick decisions. When I make mistakes, I try to learn from them, so I will not do them again. ___

 **DZ3**

I never know why some people seem to do well and succeed and it seems easy, but for me it is so hard! ___

Safety Zone **SZ3**

The battle for success requires everyone to work hard! The key is discipline in my heart and mind to practice the habits and skills that avoid danger zones and help me succeed. I will work with my VT to learn and develop good habits. ___

 **DZ4**

I spend time with people who do not have goals and who make silly choices. Sometimes I feel a little scared and wonder what will happen if I keep going this way. ___

Everyone needs help!!

 **SZ4**

I talk to my VT about making better choices and finding good people to hang out with. I write down my own goals to keep me focused.

___

 **DZ5**

When I do not know what to do, I just make a choice and move on. I do not like to talk about stuff, and I don't like people telling me what to do. I hate for grown-ups to lecture me. I would rather make my own mistakes. ___

 **SZ5**

I share my goals and dreams with trusted adults from my VT. I pray about my choices before making them, and I read the Bible to get guidance. ___

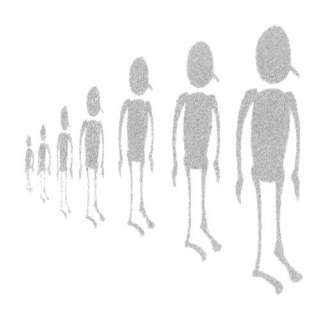

 **DZ6**

Some of my goals have failed. So, sometimes I would rather not say anything about my goals. ____

Safety Zone SZ6

Everyone has failures and disappointments. I try to be realistic about my goals. Goals take time and hard work. I keep taking small steps to make my life a success. If I fail, I pray, ask for help, and keep trying. ____

 **DZ7**

I do not like to spend a lot of time thinking about stuff. I just want to do things and have fun. ____

Safety Zone **SZ7**

It is good to have fun, but it is also important to pray and ask for God's help. I try not to make a decision when I feel tired, pressured, sad, or in a hurry. I use my preemption skills, pray, and wait until I can take time to make a good choice. Hurried decisions often cause trouble. If someone is trying to pressure me, I let them know they need to leave me alone and give me time, so I do not get into trouble with a quick decision. ____

I Have a Choice!

Group A: I have a choice! I choose to obey God!
Group B: I have a choice! I'm living by His Word!

Group A: When I obey God, God works things out!
Group B: Even when it's hard, God's way is right.

Group A: I pray and set goals; God leads the way.
Group B: I set good goals with God in my heart.

All: Because I pray!

Group A: I ask God, "Please help me succeed."
Group B: And then I pray, and His Word I read.

Group A: I spend time with God's people.
Group B: They help me learn and discern so I
make good decisions and keep my faith
strong!

Has God Helped You to See Through the Eyes in Your Heart?

___ 1. Have you learned about the following:
Spiritual Disciplines?
Spiritual Warfare?
Tricks and dangers to stay away from?

| Yes | No |

___ 2. Are you staying around people who are trying to do what is right?

| Yes | No |

___ 3. Are you letting go of violent or sexy pictures, books, movies, music, games, video games, videos, or people who pressure you to do sexy things you know are wrong?

| Yes | No |

___ 4. Do you know how to stay away from danger zones?

| Yes | No |

__ 5. Are you using self-discipline and self-control when you are tempted?

| Yes | No |

__ 6. Are you treating other people and yourself the way you know God wants you to?

| Yes | No |

__ 7. Can you act out five plans that will help you to refuse things that are not right when you are feeling pressured?

| Yes | No |

__ 8. Do you have people to talk to who will encourage you to develop good habits and let go of bad habits?

| Yes | No |

__ 9. Do you know Bible verses and stories to help you live God's way?

| Yes | No |

__ 10. Can you think of 5 goals you want to achieve in the next year?

| Yes | No |

continued

___ 11. Do you know the rules for fighting fair?

| Yes | No |

___ 12. Do you have at least one trusted, safe adult who can help you with your goals?

| Yes | No |

___ 13. Are you making choices after thinking and praying about them?

| Yes | No |

Chapter 4
Weighing Our Decisions

"Trust in the Lord with all your heart,
and lean not on your own understanding.
In all your ways acknowledge Him,
and He shall direct your paths."
Proverbs 3:5&6 NKJV

Making Decisions Can Be Difficult!

This activity can help you to make good decisions:

1. On the next couple of pages, list the choices you have for a decision you have to make.

2. Write the good things about each choice.

3. Write the difficult things about each choice.

4. Decide what is best and most important in making your decision. Discuss your results.

Choice 1:_____

<u>Good things:</u>_____

_____

_____

<u>Difficult things:</u>_____

_____

_____

Choice 2:_____

<u>Good things:</u>_____

_____

_____

<u>Difficult things:</u>_____

_____

_____

Choice 3:_____

<u>Good things:</u>_____

_____

_____

<u>Difficult things:</u>_____

_____

_____

Choice 4:_____

<u>Good things:</u>_____

_____

_____

<u>Difficult things:</u>_____

_____

_____

Practice Thinking About
How You Decide

If you have had trouble making your decision,
here are more steps to help you:

1. Look at all the facts:
   a. What do I know about each choice?
   b. Do I know enough about each choice?
   c. If not, I need to get more information.
   d. Is there a good, wise, safe person who I
      can ask for advice?

2. Think ahead:
   a. If I make this decision now, what could
      happen later?
   b. What goals will my choice lead to?
   c. Who will be affected by my decisions?
   d. How will they respond?
   e. What changes will result from my choice?

3. Think about what feelings are behind your decisions:
   a. Why am I making these choices?
   b. What feelings go with my choices?
   c. How will I feel after I make this choice?

   - Proud
   - Don't care
   - Worried
   - Revengeful
   - Confident

   - Peaceful
   - Happy
   - Don't Know
   - Confused

4. Evaluate your decision:
   Now that you have acted, review the steps above to see if things turned out the way you thought. Decide what you might do differently the next time.

This process can help you with decisions in the future!

Chapter 5
Why Some Kids Do Things That Get Them in Trouble, Part I

Fighting
Shoplifting
Cheating
Sex
Drugs

Hurting themselves or others

"Trust in the Lord with all your heart,
and lean not on your own understanding.
In all your ways acknowledge Him,
and He shall direct your paths."
Proverbs 3:5&6 NKJV

The following pages list reasons that cause some people to do things that get them in trouble.

After each reason, there is a suggestion for what can be done about it or some things to remember that could be helpful. Give your own ideas also.

Feelings

Some people are angry, frustrated, and confused!

These feelings may cause decisions that result in more confusion, frustration, and anger.

If you are frustrated, confused, or angry, try healthy hobbies and other good activities, like:

Sports	Drama	Music
Studies	Church	Politics
Mechanics	Art	Prayer
Good Reading	Talk with your VT.	Bible Study
Do something helpful for others.		

Doing these activities will help you to relax, think, and make good decisions!

Some people are afraid!

They are afraid that no one will like them for who they are.

They are afraid that they will lose a friend if they don't do what their friend does.

continued

They are afraid because someone is making them do bad things they do not like.

They are afraid because someone is bullying them.

They are afraid they will fail and feel sad.

Write some of your fears:_____

_____

_____

If you are afraid, find a safe adult whom you respect and talk about your fears.
Pray and ask for God's help.

Unloved/Uncared For

Some people do not feel loved or cared about!

Some people feel this way because they have not had someone around them who took time with them, had fun with them, and made them feel good about themselves.

As a result, they will do almost anything if they think it will make them feel loved.

If You Do Not Feel Loved

If you do not feel loved:
- ❖ Talk with your VT.
- ❖ Join a good group with kind people at a church or in the community.

God's Word will show you how much He loves you.

"God so loved the world, that He gave His one and only Son, that whoever believes in Him shall not perish but have eternal life." John 3:16

There are people within your church, family, or school who will show God's love to you by the way they treat you and give you respect.

These types of people and groups do exist!

Ask God how to find them.

Ask your VT how to find them!

Pray and keep asking for help in safe places, with safe people.

Pressured

Some people feel pressured!

They are not certain of their own ideas.
So, they are easily influenced by what
others say and do. Some people may call
them silly names and make them feel ashamed
or embarrassed because they have not had sex.

If you feel pressured:

❖ Take time to think about what is best for
you.

❖ Find safe, mature, respected adults to talk
with about your ideas.

❖ Find friends who respect your good thinking
and your good decisions.

❖ Think, pray, and take time to make peaceful,
prayerful decisions, not pressured decisions!

Confused About Sex

<u>Some are curious and confused about sex!</u>

❖ They believe having sex is the greatest expression of love.

❖ They don't realize that God created sex as an expression of love within marriage.

❖ They believe it is okay to have sex with someone even though they may break up with you at any time, because they are not fully committed to you.

❖ They are not committed to you enough to marry you.

❖ They don't know you enough and love you enough to marry you.

❖ They don't have what is needed to make a good marriage.

❖ They don't respect you enough or have enough self-control to wait until marriage to have sex.

If you are curious and confused about sex, the following may help you in developing an understanding of what you need to know about sex right now. As you get older, there may be a time when you need more information. Presently, here are some ways you may educate yourself.

1. You and your parents may discuss these issues, possibly using nonfiction books from the library or books that may be ordered from a Christian publishing company.

2. Your parents, or adults whom your parents approve, may be safe people to ask questions about sexuality.

3. Your church may have good resources for a Christian view of sexuality.

4. Christian Life Skills (CLS) discusses some issues related to sexuality in a general way during Skill 5. You may ask about ordering that information for a good discussion with your parents and/or people from your church, if your parents approve.

Instant Gratification

<u>Some don't realize that you may want something now but can wait until later to get it. They do not know about delayed gratification!</u>

❖ Sometimes God has good reasons for us to wait for what is best. Did you ever experience waiting that turned out to be for the best?
| Yes | No |

❖ Most kids who get into difficulty have not thought about these things.

❖ They believe now is the best time.

❖ They do not want to wait.

❖ They would do almost anything to have what they want now. Did you ever feel this way?
| Yes | No |

What did you want?_____

_____

_____

Did you get it right away or did you have to wait?

_____

_____

_____

Most kids who get into difficulty have not
thought about these things. Have you? _____

If you want something now:

1. Pray and ask God to show you what the best
   time is.

2. Talk to a safe adult or your VT.

continued

3. Think about what may happen if you <u>do not</u> wait, and what will happen if you <u>do</u> wait.

To be responsible and mature is to think ahead of time about choices and make decisions about the best way to manage your life.

To delay gratification is to use self-control. To use self-control is to show you are strong and self-disciplined. God will bless you for being strong and waiting for His time. God's time is always best! Self-discipline is a powerful skill! If you use it to control yourself, you will be glad that you are becoming a mature, self-disciplined person who can manage the challenges in life and not give in to the pressure of instant gratification!

Chapter 6
Why Some Kids Do Things That Get Them in Trouble, Part II

"Trust in the Lord with all your heart,
and lean not on your own understanding.
In all your ways acknowledge Him,
and He shall direct your paths."
Proverbs 3:5&6 NKJV

The following pages give more reasons for some kids doing things that get them in TROUBLE!

After each reason, there is a suggestion for what can be done about it and ideas to remember that could be helpful.

Your Ideas for
Staying Out of Trouble

Tell your ideas for the reasons some people get into trouble. Then, tell your ideas for staying out of trouble._____

_____

_____

_____

Discuss your ideas and the following ideas with an adult you trust. The person may be a parent, mentor, or minister at the church.

Being Tempted:
I Just Want to Do It!

Some are tempted to do wrong.
Some just want to!

There are times when people feel that it is harder to do what is right and easier to do what is wrong.

They may feel:

❖ It is more exciting to do what is wrong.

❖ They don't care about the consequences.

❖ It is the right thing to do because they believe everyone else is doing it.

❖ They believe they have no choice.

Did you ever do wrong for any of the reasons listed?

Yes	No

What happened?_____

_____

_____

If you feel that you cannot stop doing wrong or are confused about what is right or wrong, try this:

❖ Pray that God will help you do the right thing.

❖ Talk with an adult you trust, a parent, minister, or your VT.

❖ Think first about the results and consequences before you do it.

"No temptation has overtaken you except such as is common to man; but God is faithful, who will not allow you to be tempted beyond what you are able, but with the temptation will also make the way of escape, that you may be able to bear it."
1 Corinthians 10:13 NKJV

Resisting Authority:
I Want to Decide!

**<u>Some resist authority!
They do not like anyone
telling them what to do!</u>**

People in authority include our
parents, grandparents, police
officers, teachers, the school
principal, ministers, or others. They make
rules that guide us, protect us, or discipline us.

Some may not like the rules or think the rules
are stupid and unfair. They also think:

❖ No one has the right to tell them what to do.

❖ They are old enough to make their own
  decisions.

❖ They do not want to trust people because of
  past experiences that were not good.

If you believe people in authority are not being kind or fair:

❖ Talk to an adult you trust and ask for help when you are required to listen to those in authority.

❖ Have an adult help you find Bible verses that teach you how to manage your problem.

❖ Talk to your parent or other adult about the issues.

❖ Learn and practice skills for situations where the police or others are mean or unfair. Create skits where you practice these skills.

Not Knowing the Situation

<u>Some don't know what the situation is!</u>

❖ They may not know all the facts.

❖ They may not have taken the time to think about what they were doing.

❖ They may not know a different way to do things.

If you do not know enough about a situation, you can:

1. Try to get all the facts.

2. Ask for advice from an adult or parent.

3. Pray that God will show you what to do.

4. Think of the end results.

5. Stay away from a car or building where people may start trouble or do something dangerous. Do not get inside!

6. If you find yourself in a bad situation, get out as quickly and safely as possible; call for help!

Not Thinking Before You Decide

Some do not think clearly before they do things!

If you do not think clearly before you act, remember:

- ❖ There are always consequences to your actions.

- ❖ You need to think about what could happen if you make a certain choice.

- ❖ The results could hurt you and others for a lifetime.

- ❖ Ask someone on your VT to hold you accountable for thinking before you act.

Some believe they need to prove something!

Some try to prove they can do something.

Some try to prove they like someone.

Doing Something Just to Prove a Point

If you are thinking about proving something, remember:

❖ It is most important to prove to yourself that you can make your own best choices.

❖ If someone insists that you prove that you care for them, they probably don't respect, appreciate, or care for you just the way you are.

❖ Do not compromise your standards just to prove a point.

❖ Make sure you only do what pleases God, not what pleases people to prove a point.

You Have Power to Think, Pray, and Make Good Choices!

<u>**Some do not believe they have any real power to make choices!**</u>

<u>**Some just react instead of thinking**</u>.

If people are forcing you to make bad choices that create trouble, find safe, caring adults to help you get out of the situation. No one should be allowed to take away your power for making good choices about your life.

❖ When you are having difficulty making decisions, do this: think, pray, and ask for advice from a mature, safe adult.

Taking time to think, pray, and ask for help is what it takes to make good choices and set good goals. Do not allow yourself to be controlled by people who make you do things that you know are wrong! Get help if you need to get out of a bad situation!

Chapter 7
The Upside Down, Backwards World

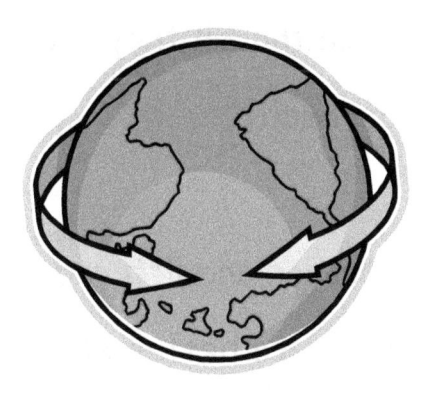

"Trust in the Lord with all your heart,
And lean not on your own understanding.
In all your ways acknowledge Him,
and He shall direct your paths."
Proverbs 3:5&6 NKJV

There Was a World

There was a world in which people did things upside down and backwards.

They smoked even though they knew it was harmful to their health.

They caused pollution and littered, even though they knew things were better when they were clean and neat.

They did not feed all the hungry people, even though they had plenty of food. And they were even throwing good food away!

They did not give houses to the homeless, even though there were plenty of places they could give them to live.

They sent millions of messages that said:

Sexual thoughts, feelings, and actions were more important than being kind, respectful, and appreciative of someone and recognizing them as a special person made by God.

They created a situation where a few people were paid a lot of money for:

- ❖ singing,
- ❖ dancing,
- ❖ comedy,
- ❖ making movies,
- ❖ playing sports, and
- ❖ selling things that looked and felt good but were not really important.

The rest of the people only got a little bit of money for more important jobs like:

- ❖ housekeepers,
- ❖ day care workers,
- ❖ dishwashers,
- ❖ nursing home workers,
- ❖ street cleaners,
- ❖ waiters and waitresses,
- ❖ food service workers, and
- ❖ caring for the elderly.

THIS IS OUR WORLD!
What are we doing about it?

Jesus said:
"The thief comes only to steal, kill, and destroy:
I have come that they may have life, and
have it to the full."
John 10:10 NIV

"The thief does not come except to
steal, and to kill, and to destroy.
I have come that they may have life,
and that they may have it more abundantly."
John 10:10 NKJV

What Can We Do About Our World?

What can YOU do?

Which of the items listed below are you able to do?

1. Make up your own mind. Think for yourself.

Yes	No

2. Do not be influenced by the crowd. Sometimes the crowd is wrong. Do what you know is right even if you are left alone.

Yes	No

3. Pray and ask for God's guidance.

Yes	No

4. Register to vote as soon as you are old enough.

Yes	No

5. Vote in all the elections, not just for president.

| Yes | No |

6. Study the Bible. Read two verses that are helpful: Ephesians 4:23 and Romans 12:1-2.

| Yes | No |

7. Work together and make friends with others who want a better world. Try to make this a better world for someone and for others who have needs!

| Yes | No |

8. Volunteer to help in a safe place, with safe people.

| Yes | No |

Chapter 8
Setting Goals, Making Decisions, Reaching Dreams

"Trust in the Lord with all your heart,
and lean not on your own understanding.
In all your ways acknowledge Him,
and He shall direct your paths."
Proverbs 3:5&6 NKJV

Making Your
Dreams and Goals Happen

If you have goals and dreams that you would like to see happen, here are some things to think about:

- ☐ Know yourself.

- ☐ Know what you believe.

- ☐ Know what is important to you.

- ☐ Know your likes, interests, dreams, and goals.

- ☐ Know what you want and don't want to do.

- ☐ Know why you want or don't want it.

Think About Your Goals

WHAT-

☐ What will it take to reach your goals?

☐ What is difficult about your goals?

HOW-

☐ How long will it take to reach your goals?

☐ How do your goals fit into your whole plan for your life?

Set Up a Plan for Action

What steps do you need to take to reach your goals?

☐ Write down the steps.

☐ Break down your goals into very small steps.

☐ Work on one small part of your goal at a time. When you finish one small part, work on one more small part!

Ask and Reach Out

WHO or WHAT do you need to help you reach your goal?

WHAT can you do NOW to move closer to your goal?

ASK for HELP or ADVICE if you need it.

MAKE friends with people who will encourage and help you reach your goal!

Think about what things may affect your goal!

What barriers might stop you from reaching your goal?

What can you do to overcome the barriers and reach your goal anyway?

What alternate plans do you have to reach your goal if something goes wrong with your current plan?

Prioritize

Think about what is most important!

Make a list of the things you want most in life. Number them in order from 1 being most important to 5 being least important.

Keep a diary or journal about your goals or dreams.

Pray about your decisions, goals, and dreams.

DON'T GIVE UP!!

If You Fail, Try Again!

Following the steps that were given to set goals and make good decisions will lead you to responsible, mature behavior.

You may have to try and keep working before you reach your goal. There are many things we can learn from our failures to help us succeed in the future.

Some of the most successful people in the world have failed hundreds of times before accomplishing amazing success! Do not give up on the goals and dreams that God gives you!

On My Own: My Battle Plan

Check the ones you will do this week:

___1. Read a Bible verse each day.

___2. Notice what influences my choices.

___3. Pray as I go through my day.

___4. Go to church and other good activities to improve my life.

___5. Think about the influences I allow in my life and my mind.

___6. Set goals for my day and for my week and try to accomplish them.

___7. If I am being pressured to do things that are not good, I will use my refusal skills to make my own choices.

___8. Notice how the media influences my choices.

___9. I will talk with good, safe people about my future goals and how to reach them.

continued

___10. I will make a list of long-term goals and steps I need to take to reach those future goals.

___11. I will think about the reasons for my choices and decisions and decide if they are good reasons.

___12. I will think about the consequences and results that some of my choices may have in the future.

___13. When I do not have the information that I need for good decisions, I will learn more and pray before I decide.

___14. I will pray, read my Bible, and try to get counsel and help from safe people so that God can help me make good decisions and choices.

___15. I will have a back-up plan for some of my goals and dreams.

At the end of the week, talk with someone about the activities you did.

Do You See Through the Eyes in Your Heart?

| Yes | No |

Do you know the answers to the following?

☐ How do you make a good choice?

☐ How do you make good goals?

☐ What influences your good and bad decisions?

☐ Who and what are good influences in your life?

☐ What are the tricks, dangers, and devices around you? How do you manage them?

☐ How do you involve God in your decisions?

☐ If you fail, should you give up on goals and dreams?

New habits and practices I need to work on:

_____

_____

_____

_____

_____

New words to help me: _____

_____

_____

_____

_____

_____

Bible verses and stories I know: _____

_____

_____

_____

_____

_____

Go back to your Strategic Plans at the beginning
of this book. Circle the parts of your plan you
completed.

Good Decisions I Can Make Now!

Below are some good decisions you can make now. Make a check mark next to the letters that could help you keep your decision and not break the promise you make to yourself.

1. I will work hard and do my best work at school by:

    a. studying my lessons on my own.

    b. reviewing my work to make sure it is my best work.

    c. asking for help when I need help or do not understand.

    d. going to the library to read good books on my own.

2. I will take good care of myself by:

    a. trying to get enough sleep and rest.

    b. washing my hands before I eat.

    c. being kind to others and staying away from danger.

    d. having good fun, getting fresh air, and exercising.

3. I will have good friends. I will save sex until after I marry by:

   a. Making friends at church, school, and other good places where people have values and standards like mine and respect my standards.

   b. Enjoying good activities with others in youth group, community programs, and other safe places.

   c. If people try to pressure me to do sexy things, I will quickly stop everything that is not right and get away!

   d. I will learn Christian Life Skills lessons about staying safe and waiting until after marriage to have sex. Then I will not worry about getting a disease or a pregnancy or other problems!

Appendix

My Accomplishments

__ 1. I read this book.

__ 2. I discussed this book with someone.

__ 3. I filled in the activities in this book.

__ 4. I have decided to continue to struggle to live for God.

__ 5. I have set good goals, and I am trying to make good choices.

__ 6. I learned the Bible verse.

__ 7. I read a Bible story.

My Name: _____

Date: _____

I discussed this book with:

_____

Certificate of Achievement
for

_____

Certificate of Accomplishment
Awarded to

_____

for
successfully completing Book 3

My Eyes' Journey
Youth Battle Plan:
Setting Good Goals and
Making Good Decisions

Date: _____

Location:

_____

_____

Signed: _____

What It Means to Be a Christian

C hrist wants to live in my heart.

H e died on the cross.

R ising from the dead, He has power to help me live for Him.

I can ask Christ to forgive my sins and come into my heart.

S ins are forgiven, and God helps me to not keep sinning again and again all the time.

T hanksgiving and praise are given to God when I go to church as often as possible.

I ask God to forgive me if I make a mistake and do wrong.

A sking forgiveness of God and others as often as I need to keeps my heart clean and my spirit humble.

N o to the bad and Yes to the good is the way I will live.

Have You Ever Asked?

Have you ever asked Jesus to come into your heart and forgive your sins? _____

When?

_____

_____

Where?

_____

_____

Are you still trying to live for God now?

_____

_____

Would you like to ask God to help you live your life for Him?

_____

Today I_____

_____

Date _____

The Ten Commandments
(Exodus 20—paraphrased)

1. You shall have no other gods except the Lord God of the Holy Bible.

2. You shall not worship any idols or anything except God.

3. You shall not use the Name of the Lord God in vain.

4 Remember the Sabbath Day, to keep it holy.

5. Honor your father and your mother.

6. You shall not kill.

7. You shall not commit adultery.

8. You shall not steal.

9. You shall not lie.

10. You shall not be jealous and lust after anything that belongs to others.

Psalm 23
(NKJV)

"The Lord is my shepherd; I shall not want. He makes me to lie down in green pastures; He leads me beside the still waters. He restores my soul. He leads me in the paths of righteousness for His Name's sake. Yea, though I walk through the valley of the shadow of death, I will fear no evil; for You are with me; Your rod and Your staff, they comfort me. You prepare a table before me in the presence of my enemies; You anoint my head with oil; my cup runs over. Surely goodness and mercy shall follow me all the days of my life; and I will dwell in the house of the Lord forever."

The Lord's Prayer
(Matthew 6:9-15)

"Our Father which art in heaven, Hallowed be Your name. Your kingdom come. Your will be done on earth, as it is in heaven. Give us this day our daily bread. And forgive us our debts as we forgive our debtors. And lead us not into temptation but deliver us from evil. For Yours is the kingdom and the power and the glory forever. Amen."

CLS Outcome Measures-Skill #3

Focus: Identifying and Using Specific Habits and Disciplines, Including Prayer and Self-Control, to Manage Decisions, Temptations, Challenges, and Lifestyle

1. Quote the Bible verses Proverbs 3:5-6, and explain what it means to you. __

2. Tell the Bible story "Two Brothers Make Choices" (Luke 15:11-32), and "Shadrach, Meshach, and Abednego Decide to Serve God" (Daniel 3:1-30). Explain what it teaches you about God, being prayerful about how He wants you to live, and how the stories can help you with good decisions and goals that please God. __

3. Describe good, safe people in your life who care about you, encourage you, and help you so that you work hard, make the most of your life, and feel good about yourself. Communicating regularly with your VT regarding goals, dreams, decisions, accomplishments, challenges, difficulties, prayer concerns, and prayer requests. These are good influences to have in your network. __

4. Demonstrate and explain your understanding of causes and consequences. __

5. Identify by name those in a positive peer group where you spend time. __

6. Tell your short-term and long-term goals and steps you are taking now to work on goals. __

7. Explain temptation, negative peer pressure, and describe or act out several ways to resist temptation and negative peer pressure through preemption, refusal skills, problem-solving skills, and prayerfulness. __

8. Describe your good, healthy habits to keep a balance in managing time, the media, self-care, exercise, eating, fun, devotional time, and good thinking. __

9. Show a résumé or a copy of the records you keep of accomplishments, goals, and decisions. __

10. Describe what you have learned from books and discussions about the way others have made decisions in challenging situations. __

CLS Scope and Sequence

	Skill 2	Skill 3	Skill 4
Memory Verse	Quote: Philippians 4:13	Quote: Proverbs 3:5&6	Quote: Matthew 28:20
Bible Story	-Daniel Has a Habit of Studying and Working Hard	-Brothers Choose -Three Boys in Trouble	-Easter story -Philip Explains the Bible
Concept 1	Practice praying, reading the Bible, worshipping God, being helpful to others.	Talk about your goals and dreams.	Learn about parts of the Bible.
Concept 2	Learn about refusal skills and self-discipline.	Talk about the consequences of your choices.	Explain how your relationship with God helps you with choices you make.
Concept 3	Know your learning style, and work and study hard.	Create a résumé.	Tell the habits that will keep you close to God.
Concept 4	Develop good habits of praying and using your mind.	Talk about the habits and choices you make when there is negative peer pressure.	Understand what it means to be a Christian with Jesus in your heart.

Additional CLS Resources

To most effectively implement CLS at your location, it may be helpful to be aware of the full range of resources available through Christian Life Skills, Inc. You are welcome to contact us for any resource listed below that may be helpful to you and/or for a site visit to assist you in developing your ministry.

- *Bible Stories that Teach Life Skills* – 1 book, all ages

- *Dancing in the Rain-Old Stories that Teach Life Skills* – 1 book, Family Resource and useful for intergenerational groups

- *Zacchaeus Climbed a Tree* – 1 book, pre-school – first grade

- *Lord, Bless Me & My Kids* – 5 booklets, parents' devotional

- *Warriors for Jesus* series – 9 books, elementary school age

- *My Eyes' Journey* series – 10 books, middle & high school age

- *Positive Alternatives Entrepreneurial Program (PAEP)* – 1 book, high risk males, ages 7-21

- *Young Adult Leadership Training (YALT) Program* – 1 book, ages 14-26

- *CLS Toolkit* – 1 book, supplementary materials for leaders

- *CLS Rite of Passage Workbook* – 1 book, culminates the *My Eyes' Journey* series

- *CLS Mentoring and Nurturing Ministry Training Manual* – 1 book

- *CLS Mentor Coordinator's Manual* – 1 book, abbreviated version of the *Administrator's Comprehensive Manual*

- *CLS Administrator's Comprehensive Manual* – 1 book

The following can support your efforts to learn about God's wisdom and good plans for your life.

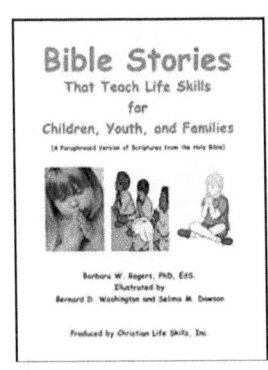 

 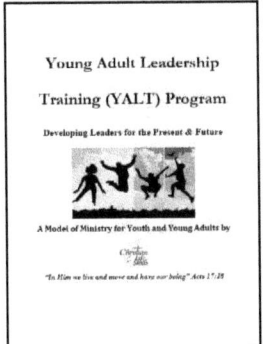 

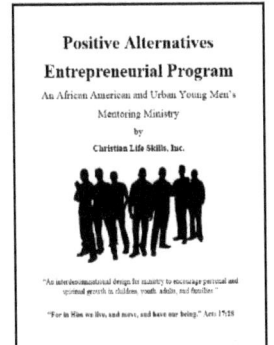 

Visit https://christianlifeskills.org to learn more about these and other publications from Christian Life Skills, Inc.